Foreword by Allen Klein, author of *The Art of Living Joyfully*

I'M SO FULL OF HAPPY TODAY

The Hygge Wisdom of Children

MARTIN ANDERSEN AND MOIRA TUFFY

For permission requests, please contact the publisher at:
Mango Publishing Group
2850 Douglas Road, 3rd Floor
Coral Gables, FL 33134 USA
info@mango.bz

For special orders, quantity sales, course adoptions and corporate sales, please email the publisher at sales@mango.bz. For trade and wholesale sales, please contact Ingram Publisher Services at customer.service@ingramcontent.com or +1.800.509.4887.

I'm So Full of Happy Today: Funny Sayings and Words of Wisdom from Kids

Library of Congress Cataloging
Names: Anderson, Martin and Tuffy, Moira
Title: I'm So Full of Happy Today / by Martin Anderson and Moira Tuffy
Library of Congress Control Number: Applied for
ISBN 9781633535480 (paperback), ISBN 9781633535497 (eBook)
BISAC category code: HUM015000 HUMOR / Form / Anecdotes & Quotations

Printed in the United States of America

CONTENTS

Foreword

ALL THINGS BRIGHT AND BEAUTIFUL: THE INCREDIBLE WISDOM OF CHILDREN

Years ago, I was walking down the street and passed a group of young kids on an excursion with their teacher. I saw one of the youngsters suddenly look up at the sky and declare in a loud joyful voice, "Look a sky line!" I looked up to see what he was shouting about and saw a white puffy line made by the jet stream of an airplane. I thought to myself, how delightfully accurate the child was. What an adult calls a "skyline" is not actually a sky line. It's the outline of buildings against the horizon. What the child clearly saw was a true line in the sky.

Kids have a remarkable way of seeing things. They are unencumbered by past events, they put together seemingly unrelated items and they enthusiastically share their new discoveries with everyone who will listen. Because of this, and so much more, I believe that children can be our best teachers. And that is why this book is a gem. In a world that is filled with false news accounts and irritating circumstances, perhaps it is time to turn to young kids who frequently tell-it-like-it-is and who often help us to laugh, no matter what the situation and often despite it.

Authors Andersen and Tuffy have done an extraordinary job of collecting the bon mots from children, both their own and others'. While this may seem like an easy task for anyone who can comb the internet for hundreds of wise and witty kid's sayings, that is not the case here. This book is a culmination of over 25 years of Andersen personally collecting those memorable words from his own offspring. And that is what makes this book so special and unlike many others that I've seen in this genre. While based on a common idea...collect the heart-warming and the humorous that come out of the mouths of the very young...these, unlike most others, are fresh, inspiring and a joy to read. Moreover, the book categorizes these charming words in like-minded thoughts. A few of my favorites are:

Logically Speaking (Justin, age 6: "Daddy, why is it called corners of the world when the world is round?").

Sooo Embarrassing (Father: "Stop picking your nose, Abigail!" Abigail, age 4: "I'm not picking my nose, Daddy. My finger is just looking!") and Blessings of Motherhood: (Isaac, age 3: "Mom, I would like to have such a big bottom like you, so I don't fall into the toilet so easily."

All in all, this book makes a wonderful read for anyone needing some uplifting, for new parents preparing for what to expect as their child grows up, and for parents and grandparents remembering the marvelous things their children once said. In other words, it makes a great gift to give to yourself or anyone who has children or was once a child themselves.

Allen Klein, author of
Secrets Kids Know...and adults oughta learn
and *You Can't Ruin My Day*

Preface

It seems that everybody is talking about "hygge" and why Danes always comes out on top in happiness surveys. We sure do "hygge" a lot, but it is such a natural part of being a Dane that it isn't something we discuss or spend much time thinking about. In fact, it is a natural as when kids say funny, cute, wise, embarrassing, and loving things.

This book contains sayings of Danish children age 3-10. All sayings have been published in a series of books in Denmark but now we thought it would be time to share them with you. I have heard from a lot of the Danish readers over the years, and just about all of them have said "We love to "hygge" with these books".

So what is "hygge"? There have been a lot of books on that subject recently, but let me try to give you a brief explanation. "Hygge" is sitting under a blanket looking out at the rain. It is having dinner at home with some good friends. It is reading a book in front of the fire. It is meeting with an old friend for a cup of coffee. It is going to the movies with someone. Well, not a very good explanation, but I'm sure you get the idea by now. In fact, I'm sure that everybody in the whole world does things like this, so most likely the main difference is that Danes have a word for it. Just like kids sometimes make up words to express something or say something that doesn't make sense gramatically, but definitely explains something very clearly. Like "I'm so full of happy today".

But enough talk – let's proceed to "hygge" with some funny and clever kids.

Introduction

"I'M SO FULL OF HAPPY TODAY!"

You read the statement above and re-read just to make sure you were reading it correctly. Grammatically correct? English not the first language? But when you realize a 3-year old girl said it you can just see her joy: a little girl who, just like a small puppy, can hardly stay still because her body is so full of life and happiness.

Children are great observers of life. They say so many funny, strange, surprising, things about everything and with an honesty that can give pause to their wisdom.

Ever since my first child was born more than 25 years ago, I have written down the funny things that he has said, and then what his little sister and their friends said. Without stopping there, I began to collect stories I heard or read about other people's children. With more than I can begin to count, this book is a collection of the best of these observations. Just thinking about each of them makes me smile and I hope that they will bring you a few smiles, giggles and a moment to reflect on their thoughtfulness.

Martin Nedergaard Andersen

Every day I am amazed by, how through their innocent observations children are very matter of fact, straight to the point and truthful with their words. They say things we wish we could and things we wish we had thought to say. They are all at once hilarious and empathic and wise well beyond their years.

We can all spend years painfully studying the great scholars, but by taking time to listen to our silly kids we perhaps might extract some of the greatest knowledge from these tiniest of sages.

I hope you enjoy some of the funny things kids say in this book and that it brings up memories of some of the things you have heard kids say. Are you willing to share some of those memories? Please share them on our Facebook page "I'm So Full Of Happy Today", we love reading them and with so much negative news out there isn't it nice that we have our children to bring us a smile every day?

Moira Tuffy

LOGICALLY
SPEAKING

QUICK COMEBACK

Mother, very firmly:
"Do you think I got "Idiot"
written on my forehead?"

Lucas, age 5: "I don't know;
I can't read!"

UH, DUH

"Well, why didn't they just look
at a globe?"

Clara Louise, age 6, when
told people once believed
the earth to be flat,
asks the question.

DIY GPS

Iris, age 4, answers her mother as to why she has drawn a big 'X' on her hand.

"It's so I know where I am."

PREVENTIVE

Rose, age 6: "I don't need to brush my teeth. I just keep my mouth shut so the bacteria can't get in."

NOTE TO SELF

Jasper, age 4, ignores his mother's requests to simmer down while roughhousing with his friend Caleb. Jasper's mother runs after the boys, and when she catches Caleb she tells him to behave properly and asks if he has learned a lesson.

Caleb: "Yeah, that I need to run faster the next time!"

FAME IS FLEETING

Aiden's picture appears in the newspaper acknowledging his 7-year birthday. His mother cuts the picture out to save it.

Aiden, sad with tears in his eyes: "Aw, now I'm not in the newspaper anymore!"

SELF-DIAGNOSIS

Jonah: "Mom, I think I'm developing a cold - I'd better get an ice cream."

Jonah, age 3, addressing his mother in the kitchen.

SOLUTION

Oliver, age 6, after spending the entire day in his room playing on the computer, his father prods him to go outside, get some fresh air and play. To which Oliver replies:

"Well, can't you just open the window?"

WHAT'S IT GONNA BE?

"Why mom at night do you and Dad want
me to lie in my bed, and in the morning
you want me to get out of bed?
Can't you make up your minds?"

Mike, age 10, at bedtime

KIDS GOTTA POINT

Justin, age 6: "Daddy, why is it
called corners of the world when the
world is round?"

LITERAL LABELING

Sarah, age 9, attempting to wash her own hair for the first time.

Sarah: "Mom, how do I do it?"

Mother: "First get your hair wet, then rub the shampoo into your hair, and then rinse it out."

Sarah: "But it says on the bottle that it's for dry hair."

IS THAT A PROMISE?

"You're never gonna pay for this!"

Taylor, age 6, furious with her father.

WHAT ELSE WOULD IT BE?

Connor, age 4, appears to have an orange hue around his mouth after eating a lot of carrots.

Mother: "What is that you have around your mouth, Connor?"

Connor: "My face?"

ROUND AND ROUND IT GOES

Samuel, age 4: "Mom, does the Earth ever get dizzy?"

A FUTURE METEOROLOGIST

"If only the trees could stand still, then there wouldn't be so much wind."

Christian, age 6, while sitting, staring out the living room window at the trees in the yard.

R.I.P.

Benjamin, age 4, is on a road trip with his family. After hitting the highway, the "vocal" GPS goes silent for a long time.

Benjamin: "Is the lady dead?"

23

MAKES SENSE TO ME

Clara, age 7: "Mom, why do I always have to go to bed at night when I'm not tired, and get up in the morning when I am tired?"

BROTHER, CAN YOU SPARE A DIME?

Nicholas, age 7, is walking down the street with his family on a Saturday morning. They pass three older Salvation Army volunteers, who are singing and ringing their bells encouraging folks to put money in the red bucket.

Nicholas: "Huh, so that's how old people earn money."

HOW TO STOP IT

Ethan, age 8, keeps pestering his parents for some new toys.

Mother: "Stop it; I don't want to listen to this any longer!"

Ethan: "Well, it's your own fault you could just say yes!"

PARENTAL CONTROLS

"Dad, how does the bottle know that it's a child who's trying to open it?"

•Addison, age 5, while holding a bottle of detergent that has a childproof cap.

INSIGHTFUL

Abigail, age 4: "Mommy, do you know why it snows?"

Mother: "Hmm no, why?"

Abigail: "It's because the clouds wants to give the kids something funny to play with."

REWRITE THE RULES

Logan, age 5, addresses his father:

Logan: "Dad, I don't wanna play football with the others any more, they're teasing me."

Father: "Well, what are they doing?"

Logan: "They keep trying to take the ball from me."

PLEEEEASE

"Mom, can I wear my short sleeved pants today?"

Christian, age 3, on the first hot sunny summer day.

DIAGNOSIS

Connor, age 3, is sitting with his father looking at a book about Egypt, comments about the image of a mummy:

"Look, there's a broken leg."

ASTROLOGY FOR BEGINNERS

3 girls, age 4, during nursery school lunch-break discuss zodiac signs:

Jessica: "I'm a Capricorn."

Taylor: "I'm a Virgo."

Ashley: "I'm a Princess."

LOCK 'EM UP

Alexander, age 5, is in the car with his father. As they drive by a prison, Alexander's father explains that is where they keep robbers and other criminals. To this Alexander replies:

"Nerds also?"

PC TALK

"Dad, look at that, they are upgrading the house."

Joshua, age 6, walking with his father, passes a house where they are building an additional floor on top.

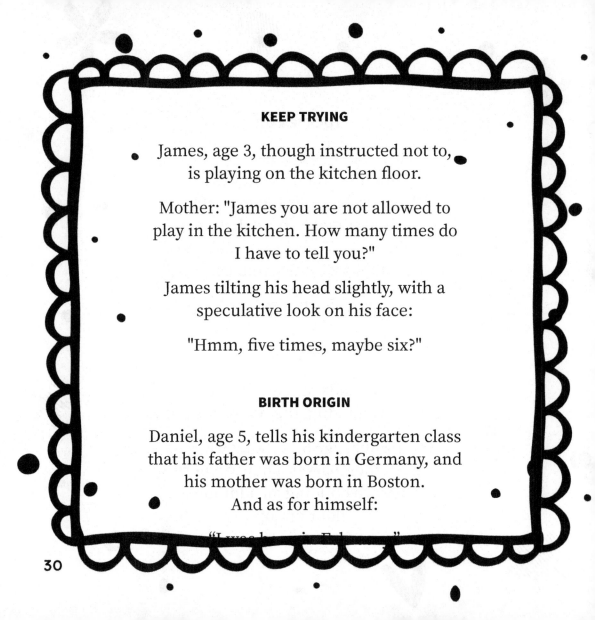

KEEP TRYING

James, age 3, though instructed not to, is playing on the kitchen floor.

Mother: "James you are not allowed to play in the kitchen. How many times do I have to tell you?"

James tilting his head slightly, with a speculative look on his face:

"Hmm, five times, maybe six?"

BIRTH ORIGIN

Daniel, age 5, tells his kindergarten class that his father was born in Germany, and his mother was born in Boston.
And as for himself:

"I was born in February."

STUFF IT

Claire, age 5, having visited a car museum
with her father, her mother asks:

"Was it fun?" To which Claire replied:

"No, not really. There were just a lot of stuffed cars."

IT STARTS EARLY

"Look, Mom, how cool! A bus with high heels."

Alyssa, age 5, upon seeing a double-decker bus for the first time.

COULD YOU BE A LITTLE MORE SPECIFIC?

Adrian, age 3: "Good morning, Mom.
What time is it today?"

TIME FOR A CHANGE

Kylie, age 5: "Mommy, when is
it my birthday?"

Mother: "June 5th."

Kylie: "No, that was last year.
This year it must be June 6th."

TOO MANY 3D FILMS

A family is on a road trip to
the Grand Canyon.

Emily, age 8, goes to the rim and proclaims:

"Oh man, that's great graphics!"

TRANSFORMATION

"When I was a little baby, I was an ugly boy. But then I got some hair and turned into a girl."

Chloe, age $3^{1/2}$, looking at a picture of herself as bald infant.

SPECIAL EFFECTS

Lucas and Brandon, both 4 years old, look at a puddle of water with an oil stain that gives off a prism effect.

Lucas: "What do you think it is?"

Brandon: "Maybe it's a rainbow that has fallen down."

NATURE'S WAYS

CAREFUL NOW

Simon, age 4, tends to fiddle a lot with his penis, so his father tells him that if he continues to fiddle with it, it will fall off.

The next day Simon is watching his mother, who's sitting on the toilet and asks:

"Mom, when did your penis fall off?"

WHAT GIRLS HAVE

Gus, age 3, has recently become
a big brother.

Gus's uncle: "Well Gus, do you like
your new baby sister?"

Gus: "Yeah - but she has two bottoms!"

FAMILY SECRETS

Kaitlyn, age $3^{1/2}$, is being brought
to preschool in the morning
by her mother.

Kaitlyn runs to the teacher and says
with a big smile:

"My Daddy farts all the time, but my Mommy
only farts when my Daddy isn't home."

LIKE LEGO

"Daddy, when you and Mom were making me who decided where to place my head?"

Ethan, age 4, after learning where children come from.

DIY

Nathan, age 4: "Where was my baby brother when I was in your belly, Mommy?"

Mother: "He wasn't born yet."

Nathan: "Well, wasn't he built yet?"

THE BIG KISS GETS THE...

Isabella, age 3, is about to become a big sister and asks her mother how babies get into the stomach.

Mother: "Well, Dad gave me a kiss and then, like magic, the baby was in there."

Isabella: "Oh, it must have been a pretty big kiss then!"

SO SWEET

Kimberly, age 6: "Isn't it good Dad that Mom gave birth to me? Otherwise, you would really miss me!"

BON APPÉTIT

Juan, age 3: "How does a baby get into the mother's stomach? Does she eat it?"

COMPUTER AGE

Grandmother: "How many children are you going to have when you grow up, Elizabeth?"

Elizabeth, age 6: "I think I'll have three. But I don't want to be fat so I think I'll just download them."

PHEW

Marcus' (age 6) pregnant Mom speaks to him about when the baby comes.

Mother: "You were born 12 days before your due date."

Marcus: "That was lucky; otherwise I wouldn't have been born on my birthday."

39 IS OLD?

"You're nice! Daddy's not, he's old!"

Clara, age 2$^{1/2}$, to her mother
who is 4 years younger than her father.

HERO*

Jude, age 5, looking
proudly at his father:

"When I grow up, I want to be
just like you Dad - just not bald!"

THANK YOU?

"Dad, I'm so glad that you're not exercising like Mom. Because then your belly wouldn't be so soft and mushy."

Celia, age 6, while snuggling with her father on the couch.

BIG SECRET

Makayla, age 4, is wrapping her father's birthday present when he suddenly knocks on her door. Makayla says:

"No Dad, you can't come in now, 'cause I'm wrapping your tie!"

SNAP!

Father: "Adam, did you clean up your room like I told you to?"

Adam, age 5: "I can't remember Dad, why don't you run up and see for yourself?"

LABOR PAINS

Dylan, age 5: "Mom, did it hurt much when you gave birth to Daddy?"

WELL WHAT ELSE WOULD HE BE CALLED?

Owen, age 3: "Mom, your name
is Ashley Smith, right?"

Mother: "Yes, and what's your name?"

Owen: "Owen Smith."

Mother: "And what about your little sister?"

Owen: "Jessica Smith."

Mother: "Yes and what about your Dad?"

Owen: "Hum, is it Daddy Smith?"

47

YOU DO THE MATH

Jack, age 5: "Mom, how
old were you when you were my age?"

SAME AGE SO...

Max, age 5: "Daddy, how old are you?"
Father: "27."

Max: "Wow, were you born the
same year as Jesus?"

DELUSIONAL

Jasmine, age 9: "At home, it's my Mom who decides. But my Dad just thinks it's him."

THANKS KID...I THINK

Emily, age 5: "Daddy, I wish you were beautiful. But I wouldn't trade you for a 100 dollars."

RESUSCITATION

Anthony, age 3, is with his father in the garage. Suddenly Anthony takes a hammer and gives his father a threatening look.

"Now I'm gonna kill you!"

Father: "No, you're not, then you won't have a Daddy any more."

Anthony puts down the hammer and hugs his father lovingly:

"But Daddy, I'm gonna blow you up again."

SO MANY TO CHOOSE FROM

"Daddy, I'm not marrying you when I grow up, I'm going to marry another prince."

Sophia, age 4, walking through the room dressed up as a princess.

DADDY'S TURF

William, age 5: "I'm in charge in my room and my Mom is in charge of the rest of the house."

Grandma: "What about your Dad? Isn't he in charge anywhere?"

William: "Yes, the garage."

JURASSIC DAD

Sydney, age 7: "Dad, you're so old you must remember what the dinosaurs looked like?"

BACK TO THE FUTURE

Benjamin, age 3: "Daddy, when you were a child like me, did we then play together?"

DADDY'S GIRL

"Why don't they have a picture of Daddy?"

Hannah, age 6, watching a news story about the world's strongest man.

TIME TO HIT THE GYM

Lily, age 6: "Look, Daddy! When I pat your belly, it makes a wave."

GO BRUSH YOUR TEETH

"Eww, Daddy – that was an old kiss!"

Grace, age 3, after being awoken by
her father with a kiss.

NOT INTERESTED

Lauren, age 5, is sitting in the living room
enjoying one-on-one time with her father.

Father: "Should we go for a walk?"

Lauren: "No, you can just open
the window if you want some fresh air."

NOT SO BAD

Bob, age 6: "Oh, you are so annoying Dad!
And you're not even very good at being
annoying..."

BRIBE

David, age 5, is sick and has to take pills, which he really hates, says to his father:

"Daddy, if you eat my pills, I will give you some of my candy."

READY FOR THE GUINNESS BOOK OF RECORDS

Sophia, age 6: "Dad, how old will you be, when I turn 30?"

Father: "I will be 65."

Sophia: "Are you crazy? That's almost 100 years!"

SOOO
EMBARRASSING...

THE DEVIL'S IN THE DETAILS

Avery, age 6, is with his father at the hair salon. He stares at a lady who sits in the barber chair next to them, getting her hair done.

Avery, loud: "Daddy, is that a man or a woman?"

Father: "Hush, that's a lady!"

Avery, still very loud: "Well, it looks like a man to me!"

POINT NOT TAKEN

Matthew, age 3, is helping his mother shop. He comments on everything and everyone. Exasperated, his mother explains to him that he can't do that and should keep his comments to himself until they get home.

While on the bus on the way home, Matthew stops to look at a man. The man smiles kindly to Matthew, who turns to his mother and proclaims loudly:

"Mom, this guy we need to talk about when we get home!"

NEED TO FIX THAT

Paige, age 3, is taking a walk with her father, when they stop to talk to a bald man who's a colleague of her father's. Paige adds to the conversation:

"Dad, have you noticed that the man's hair is broken?"

IS THAT LEGAL?

Ted, age 4, is waiting at a crosswalk with his father. While they wait an old man passes by with his wife, who is sleeping in a wheelchair. Ted loudly asks:

"Daddy, why is the man walking with a dead lady?"

911

Ava, age 5, sees a one-legged man.

Ava: "Where is your other leg?"

Man: "I lost it in a car accident."

Ava: "Then you were lucky that you still had your arms so you could call an ambulance!"

WHAT'S SO GRAND ABOUT GRANDPARENTS?

ANYBODY HOME?

"It's not fun to talk to Grandpa when he's not there!"

Thomas, age 3, calling his grandfather to say goodnight, but he reaches the answering machine instead.

IS IT A MAP?

Sasha, age 3, asks her grandmother: "Why do you have so many stripes in your face?"

SO THAT'S THE REASON

Sienna, age 4: "The brain keeps your hair in place, so without hair you don't have a brain, just like Grandpa."

BIRTH ORDER

Jordan, age 5, is at his grandfather's birthday.

Jordan: "Dad, how old is Grandpa?"

Father: "67."

Jordan: "Is he as old as you then, Dad?"

THOUGHTFUL

Josephine, age 6: "Grandma, when you get old, I'll stay right beside you. Then I can make sure that you always have coffee. And when you become really old, I'll make you a walking stick."

PERHAPS SHE DIDN'T GO TO SCHOOL THAT LONG?

Samuel, age 6, is visiting a
Toys 'R' Us store with his mother.
There are a lot of things he wants but his
mom will not buy anything for him.
To that Samuel says:

"It's much more fun to be here
with Grandma. She never learned
to say no."

GIVE ME ONE GOOD REASON

Isabella's grandmother: "You should cover your mouth when you cough!"

Isabella, age 5: "That's not necessary, Grandma, my teeth aren't false like yours!"

WEAR A WIG

Grandpa: "We're really going to play when you come to visit me this summer."

Abigail, age 4: "No, Grandpa, I don't play with anyone with bald hair!"

SOLUTION

Elizabeth, age 3, is biting her necklace, and her father says she should stop because she might ruin her teeth. Elizabeth responds:

"Well, then I'll borrow my Grandma's."

OUT THEY GO

Chloe, age 4: "Grandma, can I take your teeth out?"

Grandma: "Yeah, go ahead and give it a try, but I don't have false teeth, Chloe."

Chloe: "Yes you do 'cause you are old!"

LIMITED EDITION

"No, grandma, only at Christmas and your birthday!"

Christopher, age 4, protesting when his grandma wants a kiss.

WATCH YOUR LANGUAGE, OLD MAN

"If you do that again Grandpa you'll get grounded!"

Jayden, age 3, is visiting his grandparents and suddenly his grandfather swears loud enough for Jayden to hear it.

GOOD POINT

Andrew, age 5: "Grandpa, why do you have so little hair?"

Grandpa: "Because I'm old"

Andrew: "Well, why does Grandma have so much then?"

HAVE I GOT A DEAL

Samantha, age 5: "Grandma, do you want to trade me something?"

Grandmother: "Yes, what are we trading?"

Samantha: "I give you $1 and then you give me $5!"

SOMEDAY, MAYBE

Daddy tells Joseph, age 9, that his Grandpa is dead. Joseph says:

"I wish they had Facebook in heaven, so I could write him..."

HOMESICK

Dylan, age 2½, is on vacation with his grandparents, and he has painted on a postcard for his parents. As they put the postcard in the mailbox, Dylan asks:

"Why are we putting it in there?"

Grandma: "Then the postman will pick it up and deliver it to your Mom and Dad"

Dylan: "Can you put me in there too? I miss my Mom and Dad..."

ON SECOND THOUGHT

Peter, age 3½, while at the candy store with his mother, picked out a nice big lollipop.

On the way home, Peter runs happily while waving the lollipop and says:

"I wanna show this to Granny!"

After a little while he stops and looks closely at the lollipop, clearly eager to eat it:

"Don't you think Grandma has seen a lollipop before?"

DO THEY ALSO HAVE A PLAYGROUND?

Noah, age 5, is in the car with his mother when they pass a nursing home.

Noah: "What is a nursing home?"

Mother: "It's a place where they take care of elderly people."

Noah: "Oh, it's like a kindergarten for old people."

PART OF THE AGING PROCESS

Maria, age 4: "Grandpa, when I get as old as you, will my name also be Arnold?"

A NATURAL EXPLANATION

Austin, age 5: "I know why Grandpa has so much wrinkled skin! It's because he does not fill it all out."

ONE FOOT IN THE GRAVE

Evelyn, age 5: "Daddy, how old will you be at your next birthday?"

Father: "I will turn 34"

Evelyn: "Whoa, then you're almost dead!"

IS GRANDPA...?

The phone rings and Ella, age 4, picks it up. After listening to the caller Ella calls to her father: "Dad, there's someone called Grandfather who wants to talk to you."

THE WONDERS OF EVOLUTION

Audrey, age 5: "Daddy, your grandmother lived in the old days. Did she have fur back then?"

SOUNDS LIKE A PLAN

Cameron, age 4: "Grandpa, when my Mom and Dad grow old and are going to a nursing home, can I move in with you then?"

NEVER ASK A WOMAN'S AGE

Brooke, age 4, is grocery shopping with her mother. In the checkout line an old lady asks her: "How old are you little friend?"

Brooke: "I am 4."

Old Lady: "Oh my, are you really 4 years old?"

Brooke, angrily: "I'm not old! I'm 4!"

MISUNDERSTANDINGS OR....?

WHY NOT

Chloe, age 4 years: "Mom, could we go outside to sunbathe?

Mother: "But Chloe, there's no sun today!"

Chloe: "Could we go out and shadow-bathe?"

LOGICAL EXPLANATION

Michael, age 4, is in the bathroom where
his mother is putting on make-up.
His mother explains that she is applying
eye shadow. Michael then asks:

"Oh, is that so you don't get the sun in
your eyes?"

ANOTHER WAY TO PUT IT

"Look Mom, my lunchbox
is full of empty."

Carly, age 3, comes home from preschool
and shows her mom her lunchbox.

IT'S THE DIALECTS

Mac, age 5: "Daddy, people speak English in all countries. Things are just called something else."

DANGEROUS SPORT

Brandon, age 5, is in the car when they pass a blind man walking with a cane in the grass next to the road. Brandon observes:

"That is a strange place to play golf!"

THE TOURIST THREAT

The family is talking about what you can and cannot take, in your carry-on luggage, on a plane. Peyton, age 8, doesn't understand why there are restrictions on what you can carry onboard and her father explains that it's due to the terrorist threat. Peyton asks:

"But why do people fear them? Aren't they just travelling and taking pictures?"

IN LOVE AND WAR...

THERE ARE CERTAIN LIMITS

Sawyer, age 5, to his mother:
"Mom, I'm gonna get me a wife so you
can become a grandma, but I'm NOT
gonna kiss her!"

LOVE BIRTHDAYS

Keira, age 8: "Being in love is like having
a birthday in your stomach."

BE CAREFUL OUT THERE

Kyle, age 7: "When you're in love, you may end up getting married if you are not careful."

WHO NEEDS GIRLS

Oscar, age 3, has been Ava's boyfriend in preschool, but now it's over.

Oscar: "Ava is no longer my girlfriend, because she doesn't want to play anymore."

Father: "Have you found another girlfriend then?"

Oscar: "Yes, Hugh, because he always wants to play with me."

THERE'S A LIMIT

Milo, age 5: "I might want to have children when I grow up. But I'm not gonna have a girlfriend because that's disgusting."

FREEDOM

"Now I will enjoy my free life as a bachelor."

Joshua, age 10, after his girlfriend broke up with him.

BEWARE

Sydney, age 4:
"If you kiss a lot, you get married and pregnant."

MAY THE FORCE BE WITH YOU

Candy, age 7: "When I get married, I only want to have my husband's family name if it's Skywalker."

NOT REALLY LEGAL

Noah, age 4: "I want to have two wives when I grow up. One must have a lot of money, and the other one must have lots of children."

MUMS THE WORD

Alexis, age 7: "Mom, I've found a boyfriend at school. He is really sweet."

Mom: "Oh, how nice, what's his name?"

Alexis: "His name is Billy. But he does not know yet that he's my boyfriend."

93

THREE STRIKES...

Alyssa, age 6:
"You can only get married twice.
The third time you are going to jail."

BLECH

Aiden, age 5:
"I don't want to get married.
'Cause then you have to kiss and that's
really obnoxious."

A WARM WELCOME

James, age 5, and Hannah, age 4, are playing 'house'.

James pretends to come home from work: "Honey, I'm home!"

Hannah: "Well, go do some shopping and chop some wood!"

MIXED NUTS

CRACKING THE CODE

Ellie, age 6, comes running to her mother with a big smile:

"Mom, Mom! I can spell my name now: E - uh - a line – a line – uh a line more – E."

USE YOUR IMAGINATION

It is late autumn, and Alex, age 4, is walking by the ocean with his parents. Alex would like to take a swim, but his father tells him it's too cold. Alex asks:

"Aww Dad, can't we just pretend that it's hot?"

PRACTICAL CAR

Peter, age 2½, is in the car with his father
and the rain is pouring down.

Peter: "Dad, can the car tolerate the rain?"

Father, smiling: "Yes, it can!"

Peter, a little later: "And is it not afraid
of the dark?"

YOU MUST BE TIRED

"I'm so tired that I haven't even got
the energy to mess up my room."

Jackson, age 4½, after
having been put to bed.

THE BLIND LEADING THE BLIND

David, age 4, and Alice, age 3, are in the kitchen with their mother.

Alice: "Mom, how much is 121 dollars? Is it very far?"

David: "Yes, it is all the way out to the garden fence."

LOST IN TRANSLATION

Brady, age 5: "Daddy, how does one wave goodbye in Spanish?"

NATURE GETS IN THE WAY

Christian, age 6, while at school tells everyone that he's going to play football on the computer when he gets home.

Teacher: "Isn't it better to play outside?"

Christian: "No, the cord can't reach that far."

UNDERSTANDABLE

Isla, age 4: "Daddy, I can't clean up my room when it is so messy in there"

MUSICAL WEAPON

Felix, age 3, sees a picture of a violin and its bow.

"Wow, how cool, a guitar with a sword!"

IS IT CONTAGIOUS?

Kate, age 3, is bouncing
around and laughing loudly.
She cannot stand still.

"Oh Daddy, I'm so full of happy today!"

IT'S HEATING UP

"Daddy, why are you lying on top of
Mommy? Is she cold?"

Katherine, age 4, waking up at night and
coming into her parents' bedroom.

OUCH

Louise, age 7, has bitten her tongue: "I think one of my taste buds is broken."

DOES SHE TAKE UP EXTRA SPACE?

Natalie, age 4, tells her preschool teacher: "I'm half American, half Irish, and half human."

MODERN ART

Clara, age 7, thoughtfully looks at an abstract painting in the living room.

"Mom, I think that when the painter made that picture someone scared him up there and then he accidentally made that huge blob."

SCALE FOR SALE

"10 pounds, that is really cheap."
Sarah, age 3, standing on the
bathroom scale.

JUST SO YOU KNOW

Elijah, age 5: "Doctors are
just people who have dressed up
as doctors. They are not
real doctors."

SPECIAL OFFER

Brianna, age 7:
"If I were a toy I'd definitely
buy myself!"

KEEP THE FEELING ALIVE

Tyler, age 5, has fun sledding with his
father on the freshly fallen snow:

"Sledding is so funny that my heart gets
filled with love!"

GOOD QUESTION

Lily, age 4: "What do adults actually dream about?"

CALL THE REPAIR MAN

"Daddy, I think they forgot to turn on the lights in the TV."

Brady, age 4, turning on the TV where they are showing an old black and white film.

HUGE DIFFERENCE

Gabrielle, age 2½, wakes up
after a nap.

Dad: "Did you sleep well,
Gabrielle?"

Gabrielle: "Me not sleep,
me took nap!"

SECRET IDENTITY REVEALED

Kyle, age 8, lost a tooth and put it under his pillow with a little note:

"Dear tooth fairy/Mom, it would be nice to get a little more money than $5, maybe $10. Thanks sweet tooth fairy/Mom, Love from Kyle Johnson."

SUPER POWERS

Colton, age 6: "Jesus is tougher than Superman."

Father: "Why?"

Colton: "Because Jesus can walk on the water."

NOT A COMPLIMENT...

Bailey, age 4, is at preschool drawing but has run out of ideas.

Bailey asks one of the teachers: "What shall I draw?"

Teacher: "Hmm, how about you draw me?"

Bailey: "No, I can only draw nice things!"

PRE-CELL PHONES

Eli, age 4, is at preschool playing with a toy phone. He 'calls' his imaginary friend, Leo.

Teacher: "You can give me a call, Eli?"

Eli: "No, you're not at home!"

WHO ELSE?

Camilla, age 4, is on a bus ride with her preschool class.

As they pass the house where Camilla lives she asks one of the teachers:

"Do you know who lives next to me?"

Teacher: "No, I don't think I do."

Camilla: "My neighbor does."

NOW WHERE DID HE GET THAT IDEA?

Jacob, age 6:
"Blondes are girls who turn into monsters at night."

BYOB

Leah, age 6, is bored during her summer break. Her father has a solution.

Father: "I can play with you!"

Leah: "No, I want to play with some other children."

Father: "But I can play even though I am an adult."

Leah: "No, adults can only play like children when they are very drunk."

NEW RULES

Sydney, age 4: "What day is it today, Dad?"

Father: "It's Monday."

Sydney: "I thought it was Saturday."

Father: "No that was the day before yesterday. It can't be Saturday every day, can it?"

Sydney: "If I were God, then it could!"

ANSWER?

Layla, age 5: "Mommy, who
decided that the color red is red?"

GIVE ME A BREAK

Elizabeth, age 7, is being woken in the morning but having a hard time of it.

Mother: "Come on, you have to get up now! Otherwise, you have to start going to bed earlier in the evening."

Elizabeth, sleepy: "It has nothing to do with when I go to bed. It's just because you always come and wake me up before I'm done sleeping."

COINCIDENCE?

Tyler, age 3½: "Daddy, when will I be 4 years?"

Father: "On August 1st."

Tyler: "Oh, that's right on my birthday."

STAGE FRIGHT

Mother asks Sofia, age 4, if she wants to go to the circus (for the first time).

Sofia, looking very worried: "But Mommy, I can't do any tricks."

PROBABLY DOES

"Dad, look at the moon. It's as if God smiles at us."

Allison, age 5, up late watching the moon.

A COINCIDENCE

Belle, age 5, is visiting her grandmother in Idaho.

Belle: "Grandma, what's the name of your president?"

Grandmother: "His name is Barack Obama."

Belle, happy and surprised: "Oh how funny; ours has the same name!"

FACT OR FICTION?

Levi, age 4:
"The president, he's not real, is he?"

BEWARE

Everett, age 4, is standing in front of the
White House with his father.

Everett: "Why are the police here?"

Father: "They're looking after
the president."

Everett after thinking for a little while:
"Why, is he very dangerous?"

122

ASHES TO ASHES

X MARKS THE SPOT

"Mom, don't forget to bring
a treasure map so you can find
him again!"

Hailey, age 3, when her mom
tells that she is on her way to the
funeral of one of her colleagues.

CALL THE PLUMBER

- Caleb's goldfish died recently and instead of burying it, they flush it in the toilet after having had a small burial ceremony.

Shortly after, his grandmother dies, and Caleb, age 3, asks:

"How the heck are we gonna get her down the toilet?"

ANYBODY HOME?

"Oh how cool that there are phone numbers on the tombstones so you can call and ask how it's going."

Mason, age 4, walking in the cemetery with his grandfather.

DIED IN ACTION

Anna, age 3, sees a flagpole at half-staff. Her mother explains that it is because someone has died. To which Anna replies:

"Oh, so he didn't get the flag all the way up..."

TAKE THAT!

"Well, why am I too small to come to the funeral when I'm too big to use a pacifier?"

Sean, age 3, wanting to attend his grandmother's funeral.

UNDERCOVER

Victoria, age 5, is with her mother at the cemetery to plant a flower on her grandmother's grave. Victoria is digging when she suddenly stops and giving her mother a startled look:

"Mom, how far down is she?"

HOW WOULD YOU LIKE YOUR MEAT COOKED?

Peter, age 3, after being told by his father that when your buried the worms will eat your remains. To which Peter asked:

"When I die, will I be boiled or fried?"

127

DON'T FORGET TO SET THE ALARM

Isaac, age 5, is with his grandfather in the cemetery. They are standing over his grandma's grave when suddenly the church bells begin ringing. Isaac then asks:

"Does Grandma have to get up now?"

REFERENCE MANUAL

"Mom? Why can't we just Google if God exists or not?"

Tristan, age 5, when being told that not everyone believes in God.

SOUNDED LIKE

Rachel, age 10: "I once heard God's voice. It said Vrrrrrruuuummmmm. But it may just have been a chainsaw or a lawnmower instead."

NOT TOO OLD

Layla, age 9, has lost a tooth and put it under her pillow.

Mother: "Aren't you a little too old to believe in the tooth fairy?"

Layla: "No, do you think I'm stupid? I'm not gonna say no to the $5 you are gonna put under my pillow."

LAUNDRY DAY

Taylor, age 5: "Mom, I know why it rains. It's because God is washing his clothes."

WHERE ANGELS DARE

Jonathan, age 5, looks at a plane up high in the sky and asks what makes the white stripes.

Dad: "That's because the plane is very hot and the air is very cold so that turns some of the water in the air into a kind of a cloud."

Jonathan: "If it's that cold up there, how come angels always wear short sleeves?"

PART OF THE FOOD CHAIN

"When I die I'd rather be eaten by a lion!"

Samuel, age 3, upon being told that when you die, you can either be buried or burned.

YOU AND ME BOTH

Kayla, age 3, is in a church attending a wedding. She discovers a picture of the Virgin Mary with the baby Jesus holding a scepter in his hand.

Kayla aloud: "Oh, look at the little baby, he has an electric toothbrush just like mine."

COME OUT, COME OUT

Lillian, age 4, is talking to her mother about God.

Lillian: "Mom, is God very afraid of humans?

Mother: "No, why do you ask that?"

Lillian: "Well why doesn't he show himself then?"

DEEP IN THE JUNGLE

"Wow Dad, have you seen
Tarzan up there?"

Evan, age 4, attending a
christening in church and noticing
the large crucifix with Jesus on it.

STAY THERE

"My Grandpa died and then we
buried him and put a large stone
on top so he can't get up again."

Lauren, age 4, telling
her preschool about her
grandfather's funeral.

133

BRAVE NEW WORLD

Kaylee, age 5: "How come Jesus
is not on Facebook?"

NEVER ENDING LOVE

Robert, age 7: "Mommy, when you die I want to be beside you, in a coffin next to you. Maybe it's better if I get into the same coffin so we may hold each other."

WHEN I GROW UP...

ONE OR THE OTHER

Miley, age 3: "When I grow up, I want to be pregnant. Or a princess."

IT'S GOOD TO HAVE AMBITIONS

Elliot, age 5: "When I grow up I want to be a fireman."

Elliot's baby brother Nicholas, age 4: "I want to be God, or a Pokémon trainer."

ON SECOND THOUGHT

Nathan, age 5, is angry with his parents and wants to leave the house for good. He packs his clothes, his stuffed animals, and his toys into a lot of plastic bags and is about to leave when he realizes how much stuff he has 'packed':

"Aw, I guess I'll have to wait until I can carry it all"

DILEMMA

Allison, age 5: "I don't want any children when I grow up; I can't stand kids!"

139

DON'T WE ALL?

Father: "What do you want to be
when you grow up?"

Savannah, age 5: "I want
to be a child again."

BASED ON EXPERIENCE?

Jack, age 8:"When I grow up I don't want
any kids. They will just pester me to get
something, and I have no money."

BASIC SKILLS

Jose, age 7, in school: "I don't want to be in school."

Teacher: "Yes, you have to learn something so that someday you can get a job."

Jose: "I don't need to learn anything"

Teacher: "Why not?"

Jose: "Because I'm gonna be a policeman. They run fast and catch the thieves, and I am already good at running."

A SIMPLE WISH

Nevaeh, age 6: "When I become 15
I'd like to be a teenager."

COMMUTING

Kevin, age 5: "When I grow up, I'm
gonna get me a really cool car, so I can
drive fast to daycare in the morning."

THE NIGHT SHIFT

Isaiah, age 4: "When I grow up,
I'd like to be a ghost."

TIME TO MOVE ON

Gabriella, age 5: "Mom, when I grow up and have children, where are you and Daddy going to stay?"

HALF SMURF?

Sofia, age 3½: "When I grow up, I want to have a blue and white baby."

NO FRINGE BENEFITS

Luke, age 5: "Daddy, what happens if I become a thief when I grow up?"

Dad: "Well, you'll go to jail and you can't be with your family and friends."

Luke, after considering that for a little while: "Daddy, do you get candy in prison when you watch cartoons?"

Dad: "No, I'm pretty sure you don't!"

Luke: "Then I'm definitely not gonna be a thief!"

DICTATORSHIP

"Now I have been alive for more than seven years, and you still get to tell me what I can't do?"

Landon, age 7, is not totally satisfied with his mother.

A SURE SIGN

Justin, age 10, comes bouncing into the living room addressing his parents:

"Mom, I think I'm about to enter puberty! When I came out of the shower, I felt like setting my hair!"

WORK HAZARD

Anne, age 7: "When I grow up I want to be either a hairdresser or a cook."

Dad: "That sounds like a good idea!"

Anne: "I just wish I could be both."

Father: "Well, why can't you?"

Anne: "No, Daddy, that's silly! Then there'll be hair in the food!"

PLAN B

Gabriel, age 7: "When I grow up I want to be president."

Father: "What if you don't get to be president?"

Gabriel: "Then I want to be an ice cream salesman!"

IT ADDS UP

Emma, age 5, would like to get allowance and her father agrees to give her $5 a week.

Father: "That's one dollar for every year you are."

Emma: "Oh, I'm gonna get a lot of money when I am 50 years old."

HARD TO CHOOSE

Father: "What will you be
when you grow up, Hailey?"

Hailey, age 3: "I want to be a zoo keeper.
What about you, Dad?"

THE BLESSINGS OF MOTHERHOOD

GOOD MORNING TO YOU

"Mom? Are all people
ugly in the morning?"

Adriana, age 7, sitting on the
bed one morning waiting for her
mother to wake up.

TRUE COLORS

Madeline, age 5:
"Mother, why do you dye
your hair gray?"

SPACE AVAILABLE

Mother: "Emily, I love you
with all my heart."

Emily, age 6: "Mom, I love you too,
but not with all my heart, I have to
leave room for Daddy too."

THANKS FOR NOTHING

The family is having dinner when
Wyatt, age 5, suddenly says:
"Mom, you're old!"

Before his mother can say anything,
Wyatt's big brother Zachary, age 6,
comes to her rescue: "No, she's not
old; she just looks old!"

IT'S ALL IN THE GENES

Alexander, age 9: "Mom, if you had chosen a different man than Daddy, don't you think I would have looked better?"

TRY, TRY AGAIN

Mia's parents have been divorced for a few years. Mia, age 4, is at a birthday party holding a tiny candy frog in her hand and says:

"My Mom says that you have to kiss lots of frogs before you find a prince!"

MARK THE CALENDAR

John, age 5, has been noisy all day, and his mother has now had enough.

Mother: "John when will you stop making noise and trouble?"

John: "Hmm, next Thursday?"

YOU THINK I AM HOW OLD?

Gavin, age 7, old: "Mommy? Did you see any dinosaurs when you were a little girl?"

YOU'RE JUST MOM

Lucas, age 4, is surprised that his mother is wearing nail polish.

Mom: "It's just something that ladies use to look nice."

Lucas: "So, are you a kind of lady?"

A CHARMER

"Tell me Mom, have my arms gotten longer or have you lost weight?"

Zachary, age 9, as he gives his mother a big hug.

AFTER ALL, SHE'S USED TO IT

Jordan, age 6: "Mom, when I grow up and have children I'll live right next door. Because then you can take them when they cry."

MOMCARE

"Now you don't have to be sad anymore, Mom, I'm right here."

Liz, age 2½, after her first full day of day care.

IT'S THE THOUGHT THAT COUNTS

Avery, age 5: "Mom, I would like to find a prince for you, but I just do not know where the castle is."

A NICE WAY TO PUT IT

Mother models her new pants, for her 9-year-old, daughter.

Mother: "Do you think my butt looks big in these pants?"

Julia: "No, you do not have a big butt; it's just the pants that are a little small!"

TAKES TIME

Aaron, age 6: "Mom, how have you grown so big so fast?"

Mother: "Well, it's not really fast; I've spent 38 years working on it."

Aaron: "Wow, that's probably why you are so tall!"

ONCE UPON A TIME...

Brayden, age 5: "Mom, how old were you back in the old days?"

IT WAS MISSING SINCE JUST

Leah, age 5, can't understand why her mother is about to begin working when she has "always" been a stay-at-home mom. Her mother explains that she needs to earn money to make ends meet. To this Leah asks:

"So you mean Daddy doesn't pay you enough?"

GIVE ME A HELPING HAND, OR THREE

Alexa, age 6: "Mom, how old are you? "

Mother: "I'm 31."

Alexa looks at her hands and feet and then looks despairingly at her mother and says:

"Boy, you're old, I can't even count that far."

WATCH YOUR LANGUAGE

Aidan, age 6: "Give me a Coke, Mom!"

Mother: "That's not proper language.
You have to ask nicely."

Aidan: "Give me a Coca Cola, Mom!"

SMART BOY

Diego, age 4: "I'm in charge in my room;
Daddy's in charge in his office, and Mom is
in charge of everything."

ONLY LOSERS

Jeremiah, age 5, picks up a lollipop
off the ground.
His mother tells him to leave it there because it
is dirty and full of bacteria.

Jeremiah: "Mommy, how do you know?"

Mother: "That's something a mother knows.
It is part of the test you must take to get your
motherhood license."

Jeremiah, after thinking a bit: "Mom, what if
you fail the test? Do you then have to be a
father instead?"

THE SUPREME RULER

Jeremiah, age 5: "At my house, it's my Mom who decides who's in charge."

RULE OF THUMB

"I don't know if it's my Mommy who picks me up today. If she has a beard, it's my Daddy; otherwise it is my Mommy."

Kayla, age 3½, talking to one of her preschool teachers.

DON'T UNDERESTIMATE

Julia, age 5: "Is it hard being a Mom?"

Mother: "Yes, sometimes. A mother must cook, wash dishes, wash clothes, clean up, look after the children, and go to work every day."

Julia: "It's also hard to be a child. You have to play all day, and you can get pretty tired."

UNCONDITIONAL LOVE

Nicholas, age 4: "Mommy,
you're the best Mom in the world,
even if you have bad breath."

WHAT A GIFT

Christopher, age 7, sits next to his mother on
the couch: "Mom, today it's Mother's Day, so
you get to decide what I should
play on my Nintendo."

YUMMY

Addison, age 3½, is talking about smells with her mother and smelling various things. Eventually, Addison puts her nose close to her mother.

Mother: "Well, what do I smell like?"

Addison: "Mmm, you smell just right!"

SURPRISED

Father and mother are going to a party and are getting all dressed up. Charles, age 4, sees his mother in her nice dress and runs to his father:

"Come and have a look, Daddy, Mom is a girl!"

TRADING

Mother talks to Sophia, age 5, about love and that when you love someone very much you say that you give them your heart.

Sophia: "Can I have your heart, Mommy?"

Mother: "Yes, of course, you already have it."

Sophia: "Okay, then you can get my nose."

LOOKING ON THE BRIGHT SIDE

Isaac, age 3: "Mom, I would like to have such a big bottom like you, so I don't fall into the toilet so easily."

LOVED

Mother: "Oh, I just love you so much, Riley."

Riley, age 4: "I love me too."

ALL WORK AND NO...

Mother: "Brody, could you please go to your room and clean up in there?"

Brody, age 5: "Okay, but then I need a day off afterwards."

A PICTURE SAYS MORE THAN A 1,000 WORDS, OR...

Mother is on the floor in front of the
TV following her DVD fitness program.
Madison, age 6, enters the room and stops
behind her mother.

Madison: "Whoa, you've got a big butt, Mom!"

Mother: "That was not a very nice thing to say."

Madison: "But it is true, Mom. Should I take a
picture of it so you can see it yourself?"

172

'TIS THE SEASON TO BE JOLLY...'

173

THAT WAS NICE OF YOU, DEAR

Amelia, age 8: "Mom, last year I just pretended to believe in Santa Claus, so you wouldn't be sad."

WHITE CHRISTMAS

Dominic, age 5, wakes in the morning on December 28th, and sees that it is snowing outside:

"Wow Dad, it snows, and it's not even Christmas anymore."

BEST SEASON

Margaret, age 6: "There are five seasons: Winter, spring, summer, autumn, and Christmas."

CRIMINALS BEWARE!

Jamie, age 6: "There are four super heroes: Superman, Batman, Spiderman, and Santa Claus."

SOMETHING TO LOOK FORWARD TO

Aubrey, age 6: "I really, really look forward to the 24th of December, because then there's only one day to Christmas."

TOO MUCH TO ASK FOR

Jasmine, age 6: "Mom, what do you want for Christmas?"

Mother: "A good and sweet daughter."

Jasmine: "Hmm, then you'd better get some more kids."

TOO OLD TO BELIEVE IN MOM AND DAD

Thomas, age 6: "When I was smaller I thought it was my Mom and Dad who put gifts in my stocking. But now I know that it has always been Santa Claus."

WHAT A SURPRISE

Katherine, age 9, opens a Christmas present.

Katherine: "How cool, I didn't even know I wanted this!"

SANTA SALE

Cameron, age 5, would really like an iPad for Christmas.

Dad: "That's not gonna happen; it is way too expensive."

Cameron: "But Dad, I thought it didn't cost anything when Santa brought it?"

WHEN YOU WISH UPON A STAR

Morgan, age 4, looks through a toy catalogue trying to find things she wants for Christmas. She shows her father a toy safe and states:

"Daddy, I'd like to have this, with 5,000 dollars inside it!"

POOR GUY

Brooklyn, age 6, asks why Christmas is not in the summer.

Mother: "That's because Jesus was born on Christmas Eve."

Brooklyn: "Oh, that sucks to have your birthday on Christmas Eve. But then of course he gets twice as many presents."

SO THAT'S HOW HE KNOWS

In preschool they are talking about Christmas and Christmas presents.

Teacher: "What do you want for Christmas, Destiny?"

Destiny, age 4: "A bicycle."

Teacher: "Do you think you're going to get it?"

Destiny: "Yeah; my Daddy buys it and gives it to Santa Claus!"

SANTA'S LITTLE HELPER

It's Christmas Eve, and Santa Claus has come and just gone. Alexander, age 3, wonders:

"Was that Jesus who was just here?"

HOW DID YOU NOT KNOW?

"Oh Mom, you're just the best to find out what I didn't know I wanted!"

Addison, age 6, after opening a Christmas present.

GRATEFUL BOY

"Thank you, Grandma. That is just what I hoped to get! What is it?"

John, age 5, after opening a Christmas from his grandmother.

AD TRANCE

Brianna, age 4, is looking in a Christmas catalog from a toy store, marking what she wants for Christmas.

Brianna: "Mom, I want this here."

Mom: "Okay, what is it?"

Brianna: "I don't know until I get it!"

WORTH A SHOT

Gabriella, age 4: "Dad, could we put up our Christmas decorations?"

Father: "No, it's the middle of summer, it's a long time until Christmas."

Gabriella: "But Dad, if we hang up our Christmas decorations, maybe Santa will bring me presents?"

PLENTY TO DO

Alexander, age 4: "God is the one who created everything. So he is almost as busy as Santa Claus."

CAN'T FOOL ME

Hannah, age 5: "Grandma, I know that the Easter bunny doesn't exist."

Grandmother: "Well then who puts the Easter eggs in my garden?"

Hannah: "Oh, that's Santa Claus of course!

OR THE OTHER WAY AROUND

At Christmas Grandpa suddenly
appears in the living room dressed
as Santa Claus.

William, age 4, wondering:

"Grandma, why is Santa Claus
dressed as Grandpa?"

186

SIBLINGS

187

CHOOSE YOUR PRIZE

Asher, age 5, is going to be a big brother.

Mother: "What would you rather have? A brother or a sister?"

Asher: "A new bike!"

DECISIONS

Father: "What do you think we should name your new baby brother?"

Ryan, age 3: "Linda or Buzz Lightyear."

ENOUGH?

Olivia, age 4, is talking
with her mother who is just home with
the hospital with Olivia's baby brother.

Olivia: "Are you going to have more
children, Mom?"

Mother: "No, now it's enough, I've got
you and your baby brother."

Olivia: "Yes, and Daddy."

MARRYING DOWN

Ava, age 4: "Daddy, when I grow up,
I wanna marry you."

Big sister Madison, age 6: "You can't,
'cause you can only marry a prince."

LIAR LIAR

Ella, age 5, comes running to her mother,
yelling: "Mom! Grace is lying!"

Mother: "What did she say, Ella?"

Ella: "She says I'm stupid."

BIG DIFFERENCE

Tristan, age 5, is having an argument with his brother Cole, age 6 years. Tristan comes into the living room, crying.

Tristan: "Daddy, Cole says that I'm an idiot."

Cole: "I did not, I said you were a jerk."

BAD HAIR DAY

Sean, age 4, is at the hospital to see his newborn baby brother.

Sean: "Mom, look at him! He has just as much hair as Dad doesn't have."

DARK SIDE OF THE MOON

Bryan, age 6, is sitting in the backseat of the car with his baby sister Madelyn, age 3 years. Bryan is bothered by the sun and allowed to borrow his father's sunglasses.

After five minutes Madelyn says: "Bryan, now I want the sunglasses!"

Bryan: "No, I'm getting the sun in my eyes over here."

Madelyn: "I don't care; I'm getting the moon in my eyes over here."

DON'T TALK TO STRANGERS

Mackenzie, age 4, has just had a baby
sister and is at the hospital to visit her.

Mother: "Aren't you going to say
hi to your new sister Ariana?"

Mackenzie: "No, I don't even know her!"

CUSTOMER SERVICE

Amelia, age 4, is a bit disappointed that her new baby brother is not able to play with her.

Amelia: "He's so boring, Mom. Do you think we can return him?"

SIMPLE SOLUTION

Brian, age 5, is about to become a big brother and hears his parents talk about what they should name his baby brother, and makes a suggestion:

"Why don't we just ask him what he'd like to be called when he comes out?"

LUNCH IS SERVED

Jaden, age 3, and his father are on the way to the hospital to see his newborn baby sister.

Jaden: "Dad, we'd better bring her a peanut butter and jelly sandwich. She must be very hungry when she has been inside Mommy's belly for so long."

THREAT LEVEL INCREASED

Angelina, age 6, and Elizabeth, age 3, are playing House. Elizabeth has the role of the young child who can't behave. Angelina as the mother:

"Now you do as I say, or I will call the doctor!"

195

RETURN TO SENDER

Trinity, age 2½, has just become a big sister, but after a few days it's not quite as exciting anymore. She asks her mother:

"Mommy, when is the baby going back into your stomach?"

NOT INTERESTED

Mother: "Would you like to become a big brother?"

Christian, age 4: "I would rather be a fireman."

IF YOU DRAW IT

Carson, age 5, is in kindergarten where he is drawing a picture.

Teacher: "What are you drawing, Carson?"

Carson: "It's my baby brother."

Teacher: "I didn't know you had a baby brother?"

Carson: "I don't, that's why I draw him!"

DO YOU PLEAD GUILTY?

Blake, age 6, is playing with his younger brother James, age 4 years. Suddenly there is a loud noise followed by crying, and then Blake hurries to his mother:

"Mommy, I accidentally pushed James on purpose."

NEVER GIVE UP

Ayden, age 3½, wants his
big brother Cooper, age 6, to come outside with
him to play, but Cooper is not interested.

Ayden: "I'll count to 3, and then you come
out with me to play!"

Cooper: "No, I'm not!"

Ayden: "Okay, then I'll count to 4 instead!"

THE WORST INSULT

"I am a princess. You are nothing;
you're just a boy!"

Maya, age 5, quarrelling with her brother
Dominic, age 4.

CLICK AWAY

Mia, age 5: "Mom, can't you make me a baby brother?"

Mother: "No, Mia. First of all, I think I'm a little too old, and secondly you cannot decide yourself if it's gonna be a girl or a boy."

Mia: "Yes you can, Mom. Because the doctor has a camera that can look into the mother's belly, and if it's a girl he can just hit "Delete"!"

BROTHERS IN ARMS

Luke, age 4, has been playing with his baby brother, Evan, age 2. But now Luke sits in his room looking sad.

Mother: "What is the matter?"

Luke: "I'm just worried about Evan."
Mother: "Why?"

Luke: "Because he always cries when I hit him"

ANIMALS

A WORK OF ART

Peter, age 1½, has drawn on the wall while his father took a shower.

Father, angrily: "Oh no, Peter! What is that?"

Peter with a big, proud smile: "A giraffe!"

MIXED-BREED

Daisy, age 4: "If a Dalmatian and a Retriever have puppies which end will then have the spots?"

HUGE APPETITE

Hunter, age 3, seeing the family's two cats eating grass in the yard, becomes concerned:

"Daddy, what are we going to play on if the cats are really hungry?"

SURGEON

Austin, age 4, has cut an earthworm in two to see what's inside while playing in the yard.

Father: "That's not a good idea, Austin. You killed the worm."

Austin: "No, I was very careful when I cut it over."

OBSESSED

Clara, age 7, can't sleep because she keeps thinking of a hamster that she would really like to have. Her mother suggests that she tries to count sheep.

Clara: "I've already tried, but they keep turning into hamsters."

STAY THERE

Adrian, age 8, tosses and turns and can't fall asleep. Daddy tells him to try counting sheep and tells him how to do it.

After 5 minutes Adrian yells:

"I can't count the sheep, they won't stand still!"

SERIOUSLY LADY

Connor, age 6, is watching two birds on top of the school roof and asks the teacher what they are doing up there.

Teacher: "They are probably looking for worms."

Connor: "Hello! There aren't any worms on the roof!"

NEW BREED

"Oh look, a teddy bear dog!"

Owen, age 2½, passing a poodle as he is out walking with his parents.

CLEARED

Peter, age 3, is visiting
his grandmother but cannot
find his toy gun.

Dad, jokingly: "Have you checked
if the cat has taken it?"

Peter, a little later: "No, look at its
paws, there's nothing there."

OUCH

James, age 5, is watching a snail creep across the road.

James: "Daddy, do snails have penises?"
Father: "I do not know, why?"

James: "Well, it's gotta hurt when they crawl on it like that."

UNDO, PLEASE

Clara Louise, age 5:
"If only God hadn't created spiders...!"

TRAFFIC SAFETY

Madelyn, age 5, is out riding her bike with her mother.

Madelyn: "Oops, I just ran over a snail."

Mother: "That's a shame."

Madelyn: "Yeah, well it could just have looked before it ran out onto the road."

GENDER LESSON

Olivia, age 5, is talking on the phone with her grandfather: "Grandpa, I've got a new dog!"

Grandpa: "Great, what's its name?"

Olivia: "Charlie."

Grandpa: "So it's a boy."

Olivia: "No grandpa, it's a DOG!"

LACK OF FOCUS

Andrew, age 3, is at the zoo with his grandparents. The tigers just had cubs, and Grandpa lifts Andrew up so he can get a better view. Andrew observes:

"Oh look, there's a duck!"

PARENTAL GUIDANCE RECOMMENDED

Leon, age 8, has been to the aquarium  with his school class and comes home very excited and tells his mom about the fish:

"Mom, there were some fish that were completely transparent, so you could see all of their orgasms."

HEALTH WARNING

On the way into the supermarket Owen, age 4, sees a sign showing a dog with a red line crossing through it (the international sign for 'no') and says:

"Look Dad, dogs shouldn't smoke in here."

BATH TIME

Aubrey, age 4, is visiting her grandparents and is looking at their aquarium.

Aubrey: "Have you got new fish, Grandma?"

Grandma: "No, they're the same ones we had last time you were here."

Aubrey: "They look so beautiful with all of those colors. Did you wash them?"

HOMELESS

Kaylee, age 4, while walking with her mother, finds an empty snail shell on the ground:

"Do you think the snail can find back home again?"

ROYAL RANKS

Kim, age 3, is picked up by her mother from day care.

Kim: "We saw a very big bee in the playground today."

Mother: "Well, it was probably a queen bee."

Kim: "Yeah, or maybe a princess bee."

THE EYE OF THE TIGER

Anna, age 4, is painting a picture of a tiger but will not paint the eye.

Mother: "Why don't you paint the eye?"

Anna: "Because then it can't see anything."

COME AND GET IT!

FAVORITE DISH

During the 1st graders lunch break the teacher asks the children their favorite foods.

Luis: "Hamburgers."

Zoe: "Salmon."

Peyton: "Pizza."

Juan: "My mother!"

EXOTIC

Brooke, age 4, is sitting in
the backseat of the car, with her friend
Kaitlyn, as they drive past a field of cows.

Brooke: "Wow, look at all those horses."

Kaitlyn: "They're not horses; they're cows.
They're the ones we get milk from."

Brooke: "Oh, you're so lucky; we get our
milk from the supermarket."

BORING

"They don't taste like much, they are
probably healthy then."

Chase, age 7, on tasting some new cookies
that mother brought home.

WORK-AROUND

Evelyn, age 5, is
visiting her neighbor.

Evelyn, quietly: "My Mom says
I can't beg for ice cream."

After a bit she continues:
"But if you ask me if I want some
it's okay for me to say yes."

MISUNDERSTANDING

Layla, age 6, is at the zoo with her father where they see a cow being milked.

In the car on the way home, Daddy says:

"So now you know where the milk comes from."

Layla: "Yes, it comes from the Zoo."

UNHAPPY MEAL

Jason, age 9, says while at McDonalds: "I want a cheeseburger without cheese."

HAVING WHAT FOR DINNER

Kimberly, age 5, comes into the kitchen where her mother is just about to put a whole chicken into the oven.

Kimberly: "Yecch, why have you peeled a frog, Mom?"

BEST CHEF

Julian, age 4, is cooking for his father on his toy stove.

Julian serves his father the 'dinner':

"Here you go, Daddy! I've made your favorite foods: Chocolate and red wine."

THESAURUS

The twins Wyatt and Carter, age 6, have different eating habits; Wyatt eats only meat and Carter (believe it or not) eats only vegetables.

Dad: "So that means that you are a vegetarian, Carter."

Wyatt: "Well, then I guess I'm a meatatarian."

MANY VARIETIES

Charles, age 5, has been shopping with his mother:

"Me and Mom have bought three different kinds of apple juice: One with mixed fruit, one with oranges, and one with apples."

EAT TO EXHAUSTION

Josiah, age 5: "Mommy, I can't eat any more; my arms are too tired."

BACK IN THE DAY

"Mom, did I like Chinese food when I was a child?"

Addison, age 4, during dinner.

EFFECTIVE SOLUTION

Logan, age 5, comes in from
the garden after having played all morning:

"Phew, I'm sweaty, Mom!"

Mother: "Then take off your jacket."

Logan, a little later: "It doesn't help really.
I think it's best if I get an ice cream."

THAT'S THE WHOLE POINT

Morgan, age 5, is shopping with her grandma and wants some candy.

Grandma: "Why don't we buy some apples and bananas instead?"

Morgan: "No, Grandma, they're not unhealthy!"

LITTLE FINGERS

Ava, age 5: "Mom, how do they get the stones into grapes?"

BAD HABITS ARE HARD TO BREAK

Matthew, age 4, is having dinner with his parents, but he is carefully avoiding his carrots.

Father: "Why don't you eat your carrots, Matthew?"

Matthew: "I have quit eating carrots, just like when you quit smoking, Dad."

EASY SOLUTION

The family is having dinner and again Angelina, age 5, says that she doesn't like the food.

Father: "Just think of the small children in Africa. They would be happy to eat it, because they have almost no food."

Angelina: "Well, why don't they just take something from the freezer?"

IT'S A TASTE THING

Ethan and Landon, both 4 years old, are sitting and talking together on the playground.

Ethan: "Yecch, are you eating your boogers?"

Landon: "No, I spit them out again, 'cause they taste like cheese."

DIFFERENT PRIORITIES

Father: "I love you very much, Taylor."

Taylor: "I love ice cream."

DANGEROUS VEG

Natalie, age 5: "Mommy, do you cry when you cut tomatoes?"

Mother: "No, that's only when you cut onions."

Natalie: "Yeah, tomatoes are not as dangerous as onions."

AVOID AT ALL COSTS

Lillian, age 5, reluctantly tastes the new dish that her mother has cooked.

Lillian: "It tastes like squirrel, Mom!"

Mother: "Well, how does squirrel taste?"

Lillian: "Not very good..."

FREEZING

"Oh, Grandpa, the ice is so cold that I got goose bumps on my teeth."

Nicholas, age 4, while eating a large ice cream cone.

ACCIDENT?

Claire, age 4, while eating dinner, spills her glass for the third time.

Dad: "Come on Claire, you have to be more careful!"

Claire: "Sorry, Dad, it was not an accident."

REALLY THIRSTY

"Daddy, I'm so thirsty that I'm just about to pee my pants."

Samantha, age 4, after getting home from a long day at preschool.

CALL THE DOCTOR

HEALTH WARNING

Brady, age 7: "Dad, is motion sickness contagious?"

GOOD EXCUSE

Victoria, age 4: "Mom, I can't help you take out the dishes! I have a bad headache in my leg."

LOOK OUT

Liam, age 3, has been sick in day care, and his mother comes to fetch him.

Mother: "Oh, sweetheart, do you feel really bad?"

Liam, sobbing: "Yes."

Mother: "Does it hurt anywhere?"

Liam stops and points down at his feet: "Yes, there! You stepped on my foot, Mom!"

THAT CAN BE PRETTY DANGEROUS

Hayden, age 7, wakes up
not feeling well:

"Mom, I think I'm sick.
I haven't breathed all night."

RARE DISEASE

Nathaniel, age 3, after being asked to
help clear up the toys in day care says:

"I can't, because I have a
cold in my eyes."

NOT SO DANGEROUS AFTER ALL

Henry, age 5, tells his kindergarten class that he is going to the doctor to get a vaccination.

Teacher: "Oh, my!"

Henry, reassuring: "Don't worry, he takes the needle out again!"

PLUG IT IN

Ian, age 3½, threw up in his bed overnight, and when his mother comes into his room says:

"Mom, I won't throw up on you 'cause I have a "paci" (pacifier) in my mouth."

239

UNHAPPY ENDING

Claire, age 5: "Daddy, would you rather lose your arms and legs or die?"

Father: "Hmm, that's not an easy question, because without arms and legs it is not certain that you will have a very good life."

Claire: "No, because if you have no legs, you will fall over and break your neck and then you die!"

SOUNDS REASONABLE

"Mom, I can't see out of my nose."

Maria, age 5, has a very bad cold, and her nose is completely blocked.

OUCH

Hailey, age 4:
"Oh, I have a headache all
over my body!"

SAY WHAT?

Jonathan, age 5, has an infection
of the middle ear and goes to see
the doctor.

Doctor: "Well, what's wrong
with you, Jonathan?"

Jonathan: "I have lost my voice
in my ear."

SCHOOL'S OUT

HIGH EXPECTATIONS

Stella, age 5: "Daddy, I don't want to start school after summer, I can't read or write."

SMALL PRINT

Ashley, age 4, is sitting at her dad's computer typing. It's just a lot of jumbled letters, but when she is finished she prints it out and shows it to her Father.

Father: "Can you read what it says, Ashley?"

Ashley: "No, not without glasses."

A TRUE FRIEND

Gabriel, age 6, comes home from school with very red eyes.

Mom: "Have you been crying, Gabriel?"

Gabriel: "Yeah, Nathan's grandfather died and I helped him cry."

LETTERS OR NUMBERS?

"Um, I think it starts with a seven?"

Brody, age 6, has just started 1st grade, and the teacher asks if he can spell his own name.

DISCLOSURE

Rebecca, age 6, just started school and tells her baby brother Isaac, age 4, about it.

Isaac: "I also started school."

Rebecca: "Well, may I see your school books then?"

Isaac: "No you can't, 'cause I've forgotten them in kindergarten."

HE'S GOING SOMEWHERE

Xavier, age 9, is talking to his father about school.

Father: "So Xavier, are you the best in your class?"

Xavier, after thinking for a moment: "No, but I am the best at cheating!"

A SIGN OF WISDOM

Jessica, age 5: "When I start in school I'm gonna be so clever that I need glasses just like my Mom."

DO OVER

Adam, age 6, is looking forward to starting school after the summer.

Adam: "Mom, when we start in school, who would you like to sit next to?"

SAY WHAT?

Carlos, age 7, is not so very good at paying attention in class.

Teacher: "Do you have dirt in your ears?"

Carlos: "Nah, it's just a little sand."

STUPID QUESTION

Sebastian, age 8, comes home from a school trip to the local museum.

Mother: "Was it a good trip?"

Sebastian: "Yeah, guess so."

Mom: "Did they have anything new?"

Sebastian: "No Mom, it's a museum; they only have old stuff!"

TIRED OF SCHOOL

Tyler, age 7: "I don't wanna go to school anymore. I'd rather retire right away!"

WORDS OF WISDOM

Nathan, age 6: "Now I know my addition and subtraction numbers 1-10 so now I want to learn the C's."

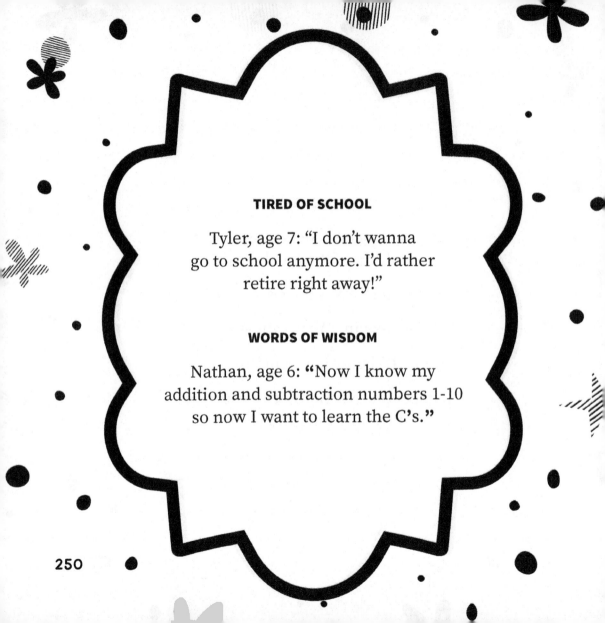

WHO?

The teacher asks if the students know who the first two people on earth were.

Victoria, age 6: "Hansel and Gretel."

Anthony, age 6: "No, it was Adam and Steve".

HOPEFULLY BOTH

Isaiah, age 8, has been at the Zoological Museum with his school class and tells that he has taken a picture of a bear.

Father: "Was it dead?"

Isaiah: "No, it was just stuffed."

NOT ENOUGH

The 4th grade English students are asked to write a short essay about what they would do if they suddenly had a million dollars.

After 20 minutes Gavin, age 9, raises his hand and asks: "Could I get 100,000 dollars extra?"

IS THAT A CRIME NOW?

Amelia, age 6, raises her hand in her 1st grade class.

Teacher: "Yes, what would you like to say, Amelia?"

Amelia: "Nothing, I was just pointing at the ceiling."

MATH'S HARD

Mother and Jordan, age 6, are playing a board game where you have to add or subtract numbers. Jordan has not learned to subtract yet, so Mom suggests that they just add.

Jordan: "I know how to subtract."

Mother: "Okay then, what is 5 minus 2?"

Jordan: "Dog?"

AUTHOR'S BIO

Martin N. Andersen is a full-time inventor of board and card games; the good old-fashioned physical kind of games, that is. During the last six years, Martin has licensed more than 200 games to companies in 20 countries all over the world.

Besides making games, Martin has authored or co-authored 10 books. He also has an MBA and is an associate professor at Edinburgh Business School.

Martin is born in and still resides in Copenhagen, Denmark, with his wife, daughter, and three cats, but he tries to spend at least 1-2 months in the US each year, visiting game publishers and looking for book inspiration, but mostly just because there are so many great places to visit.

Moira is a communications and marketing professional who has done time between the corporate, agency and freelance worlds supporting multiple sectors including energy, real estate, music, not-for-profit, hospitality and toys and games. After years of corporate writing and being a keen observer language, especially that of her young nieces, led Moira to stray into some lighthearted writing. "I Am So Full Of Happy" is Moira's first co-authored book. She has written articles for a number of food-centric online publications, including her own blog: To Market with Mo. Moira balances the cerebral by teaching yoga and fitness in the city of Chicago where she lives with her husband and her 'nanny' aka her Great Pyrenees, Gigi.

CPSIA information can be obtained
at www.ICGtesting.com
Printed in the USA
BVOW09s2332110617
486564BV00002B/3/P